SEASONS

Spiritual Meditations For Winter, Spring, Summer, and Fall

Christine A. Adams

TABLE OF CONTENTS

Copyright _____ 5
Dedication _____ 6
Winter _____ 9
    1. "Be Grateful For What You Have" _____ 11
    2. "Acceptance Brings Serenity; Serenity Brings Happiness" ____ 12
    3. "Peace Is The Ultimate Happiness" _____ 13
    4. "Love Yourself As God Loves You" _____ 14
    5. "Speak To Yourself As A Loved Child" _____ 15
    6. "Forgive And Heal Yourself" _____ 16
    7. "You Can Choose To Heal" _____ 17
    8. "Admit To Weaknesses" _____ 18
    9. "Deal With Your Anger" _____ 19
    10. "Find Out Where Your Anger Comes From." _____ 20
    11. "Detach With Love" _____ 21
    12. "Build A Community Of Love" _____ 22
    13. "Share Your Gifts" _____ 23
Spring _____ 28
    1. "You Are The Hero Of Your Life" _____ 30
    2. "God's Will For You Is Joy" _____ 31
    3. "Listen To Your Inner Voice" _____ 32
    4. "There Is An Infinite Abundance Of Love" _____ 33
    5. "Dedicate Your Life To God And Serve Others" _____ 34
    6. "Put First Things First" _____ 35
    7. "Keep It Simple" _____ 36
    8. "Forgiveness Is Your Primary Function' _____ 37

9. "Find Peace By Forgiving Your Parents" _____ 38
10. "Breathe, Step Back And Reflect" _____ 39
11. "Find Time To Pray" _____ 40
12. "Be Still And Know God" _____ 41
13. "There Is Always A New Day -A Second Chance" _____ 42

Summer _____ 47

1. "Holy Relationships Are Possible" _____ 49
2. "True Love Is A Decision" _____ 50
3. "Find The Wonder In Relationships" _____ 51
4. "Work On Understanding Another's Point Of View" ___ 52
5. "Let Go Of Your Problems" _____ 53
6. "Don't Insist On Being Right. Be Happy!" _____ 54
7. "Honesty Is The Best Policy" _____ 55
8. "You Can Be A Messenger Of Love!" _____ 56
9. "Rejoice In Each New Day" _____ 57
10. "Rituals That Give Symbolic Meaning To Your Life" ___ 58
11. "You Are Not Alone" _____ 59
12. "Believe There Is Nothing To Fear" _____ 60
13. "Look For Self 'Within' Not Outside Of You" _____ 61

Autumn _____ 66

1. "Remember God's Love Is Permanent" _____ 68
2. "A Kind Word Can Change A Life" _____ 69
3. "Listen With Your Heart" _____ 70
4. "Your Spiritual Job Is Your Most Important One" _____ 71
5. "Fear Drives Out Faith" _____ 72
6. "Make Peace Your Goal" _____ 73
7. "No One Can Make You Happy But Yourself" _____ 74
8. "Avoid All Extremes" _____ 75
9. "To Give Is To Receive" _____ 76

10.	"Honor The Sacred Nature Of Relationship"	77
11.	"Your Thoughts Can Heal Or Harm Others"	78
12.	"When One Door Closes Another Opens"	79
13.	"The Journey Is The Final Answer"	80

Also by Christine A. Adams _____ 84

"Spirituality: A Life Force" _____ 85

Chapter One: Spiritual Teaching _____ 87

ABC's of Grief by Christine A. Adams! _____ 102

Copyright

First Edition

Copyright © 2021 Christine A Adams

All rights reserved.

Published by Hanley-Adams Publishing – 2021

ISBN 13: 978-1-7345727-5-9

All rights reserved. No part of this book may be reproduced or utilized in any form or by any means, electronic or mechanical, including photo-copying, recording or by any information storage or retrieval system, without permission in writing from the publisher. Printed in the United States of America.

The ideas presented herein are the personal interpretation and understanding of the author and are not endorsed by the copyright holder of A Course in Miracles.

Portions from A Course in Miracles ©1975, Reprinted by Permission of the Foundation for Inner Peace, Inc., P.O. Box 1104, Glen Ellen, California 95442.

Dedication

To my loving husband:

Robert J Butch who died on January 7, 2021. I wish to acknowledge his steady support of me, his unwavering love, and his inspiring example of courage and spirituality. Without him, nothing of what I have written these past 30 years would have been possible.

To my talented son:

Mark D. Hanley who edited, format and published this book, as well as his own techno thrillers, Bit by Bit (2019) and Carbon Copy (2020) for his creative intelligence, his persistence, and his conscientious dedication to writing and publishing - as well as his never ending concern for family.

To my ever caring daughter:

Marcia Firsick, and her husband, Mike Firsick, and their two sons, James and Ben, for their love and support for me and Bob during these two difficult years. Without them, I would not have survived the pandemic and this book would not exist!

To my eldest son:

Edward T. Hanley, and his wife, Michelle as well as their children Harrison and Grace for their constant support every day, every year. A special thank you to my grandson, Harrison Hanley, for his iconic photography, which provided the cover images for my last three books. (See at www.harrywander.com.)

Winter _____ 9
1. "Be Grateful For What You Have" _____ 11
2. "Acceptance Brings Serenity; Serenity Brings Happiness" ____ 12
3. "Peace Is The Ultimate Happiness" _____ 13
4. "Love Yourself As God Loves You" _____ 14
5. "Speak To Yourself As A Loved Child" _____ 15
6. "Forgive And Heal Yourself" _____ 16
7. "You Can Choose To Heal" _____ 17
8. "Admit To Weaknesses" _____ 18
9. "Deal With Your Anger" _____ 19
10. "Find Out Where Your Anger Comes From." _____ 20
11. "Detach With Love" _____ 21
12. "Build A Community Of Love" _____ 22
13. "Share Your Gifts" _____ 23

Winter

The Winter Season

The winter season centers on gratitude-on being grateful for what we have. We know that gratitude has nothing to do with an abundance of material possessions. There are people who have many riches but can't find gratitude in their hearts; but there are those who have nothing but who are thankful for the simplest thing. It is a matter of perspective!

November and December signal that the year is coming to an end. As we enter this somber winter season it gets darker and colder in many climates. It's the time for Thanksgiving, a time for reflection and Christmas, a time of rebirth.

As the year ends, we celebrate where we have been and where we may go next year. Initially, gratitude doesn't just happen. It's an attitude that comes from the acceptance of self, and, ultimately, acceptance of life itself as it unfolds, and acceptance of God's place in our lives. Once again, it is crucial to our peace of mind that we come to understand and accept ourselves as children of God. With this identity, we recognize our spiritual essence which transcends our physical self.

When the last fall flowers fade and give way to death, we grieve all those loved ones we have lost. We miss their presence, their warmth and love and we are reminded that someday we, too, will die. In the cold of winter without the light of summer sunshine, without the abundance, or a time of growth, a dark despair can creep into our life unless we consciously nurture an attitude of hope and gratitude by remembering God's Love.

Most importantly, we will need to accept life on life's terms- not on our terms. When we see ourselves as a victim, or live by our own will-that is by having expectations of life, we will surely be unhappy. We are not an all knowing God who can direct our lives at will.

Expectations are really demands that we make of life, of God. When they are not fulfilled, we become discontent. We lose sight of what we do have by concentrating on what we do not have. We deny our spiritual perfection and forget that God's Love is a love that surpasses all human understanding!

1. "Be Grateful For What You Have"

Thank God for the good things in your life. Gratitude implies acceptance and leads to inner peace. You can find gratitude in the events of your everyday life.

Be thankful when it is below zero and the car starts, or when you can see the bright colors of Christmas, the whiteness of snow and the power of the ocean. When a friend walks beside you, holds your hand, hears your words and responds gently; when there is silence without loneliness, and noise without confusion.

You can find gratitude for health, for family, for the ability to work, to walk, to speak, to love one another, to be loved. Be thankful for life, for nature, for the ability to laugh, for the ability to feel, to be sad, to be angry, or to be afraid. Collect these gratitude moments every day and at the end of the day thank God for his goodness. Everyone has something to be grateful for - even if it is just being alive.

When things seem to be going wrong, don't think of how little you have, think of how much you have. Give God a chance! Robert Herrick once said, "Thanksgiving for a former (benefit), doth invite God to bestow a second benefit." So, make a gratitude list today!

An attitude of gratitude becomes a way of life. When you are grateful for what you have, you attract more blessings in the form of increased prosperity and happiness, a fulfilling life work, or satisfying personal relationships. The more you feel grateful, the more reasons you find to feel it. It is like a magical magnet attracting love, joy and peace.

Gratitude goes hand in hand with love,
and where one is the other must be found.
ACIM Work book page 363

2. "Acceptance Brings Serenity; Serenity Brings Happiness"

With gratitude and acceptance, we can prepare for "miracles" which are those good things that happen when we least expect them to happen.

We may not understand Divine Providence in all situations but when we look back on our life, we see that some good has come out of a seemingly bad situation. We could never have foreseen this positive outcome.

We need not rebel. When we accept God's will and "Let Go and Let God", the load drops from our shoulders and the assurance that "all will be well" brings peace to our soul.

Sometimes, we have the wrong perspective about happiness. We think it comes from the pursuit of our wants and desires, and the avoidance of pain and suffering. Actually, happiness comes from serenity, from conforming our will to the Will of God.

God, grant me the serenity to accept the things I cannot change, the courage to change the things I can, and the wisdom to know the difference.

3.   "Peace Is The Ultimate Happiness"

With acceptance and the gratitude, we realize it isn't so much what is happening to us, but how we handle it. We are open to seeing good when we are <u>not</u> closed off from God. If we refuse to see any good, we will be unhappy.

You can be happy. It's up to you. Gratitude and acceptance will bring you peace. The formula is simple, yet paradoxical, because we need acceptance of ourselves, and the events of our life to be grateful. We need gratitude to find peace of mind and we need peace of mind to be really happy.

This winter season, let us praise and celebrate life not as a victim but as a victor. One who accepts all things with gratitude understanding that God loves us and never leaves us. For that, we can be eternally grateful!

"Let Go and Let God"

4. "Love Yourself As God Loves You"

When you keep a spiritual perspective through faith, you can love yourselves as God loves you. It would be hard to conceive of the energy of God's love as a conditional force - a love which picks and chooses special people to love. Therefore, you are asked to forgive yourself and love yourself unconditionally, as God loves you.

Until you love yourself unconditionally, it is difficult to love another. So it has to start with you. First, be gentle with yourself. Give yourself permission to grow.

Everything takes time. Therefore, give yourself the time you need to love yourself. When you forgive yourself, you lift a great weight from your own shoulders. All of us are at the right place for this moment. Give yourself permission to grow and to come to the awareness of life. What's your hurry? Be kind but not indulgent. Be good to yourself. You are God's child.

Be kind to your mind. Fill it with positive affirmations. Don't abuse your mind with negative thoughts. Be kind to your mind by praying, meditating, and visualizing positive outcomes.

Stop criticizing yourself. Don't beat yourself up with words like "bad", "dumb", or "worthless". You are God's child. And finally, stop scaring yourself. You do not need to be afraid. Fears of abandonment and rejection are not real. When you rely on the power and love of God, there is nothing to fear!

God is the love in which I love myself,

God is the love in which I am blessed.

ACIM Lesson 46

5. "Speak To Yourself As A Loved Child"

In <u>Illuminata</u>, Marianne Williamson says, "one light seems small and weak, but no one's light is ever alone, for all your lights are part of God." Today, praise God who in his Infinite Wisdom made you his child.

It is your right and duty to accept your place in the universe. No, it is not arrogant to understand the power of your own spirit and connect yourself to God. Rather, it is prideful to think you are separate - some special being that operates in your own sphere. Unlike anything else in the universe.

Praise yourself. Don't listen to your own negative self-talk. Use positive affirmations to strengthen your true self - your spiritual self. Tell yourself "I am God's child". Not once but all the time. Talk to yourself as a loving God would talk to His child.

Be imitators of God, therefore, as dearly loved children.

Ephesians 5:1

6.   "Forgive And Heal Yourself"

The author, Gerald Jampolsky, wrote in <u>Love Is Letting Go Of Fear</u> "Forgiveness is the vehicle used for correcting our misconceptions and for helping us to let go of fear. Simply stated, to forgive is to let go".

For example, if your relationship with your parents is or was troubled, you need to drop your defenses, your pain, and allow the healing process to happen. Ultimately, you can only find peace by forgiving your parents for not being perfect.

First, make a list of all the things you resented about your parent. Be specific. Use creative visualization by imagining your parent hearing you state these resentments, acknowledging your pain, accepting your feelings. Visualize you and your parents together covered with a warm, radiant light. Let this be the reconciliation of God's love.

Forgiveness is the way to peace of mind. Why hold back? Some people think forgiveness is a concession to those who have harmed us. It isn't! Forgiveness is always a gift to you. Release of another person is release of self.

Give yourself the gift of forgiveness. The reconciliation between you and your another person has already taken place in the mind and heart of God. It is only a matter of time until you catch up whether it be in this world or the next.

Bear with each other and

forgive whatever grievances

you may have against one another.

Forgive as the Lord forgave you.

Colossians 3:13

7. "You Can Choose To Heal"

Peace of mind comes to those who chose to heal and not to judge. Whenever you make a conscious choice to forgive, to heal a situation, you are giving the gift of peace to yourselves as well as the other person.

It is like a circle where the peace you give comes right back to you. Giving and receiving are one - could there be a better gift than the gift of healing?

There is a visible difference between an unforgiving place and a forgiving one. You can see the frantic, distorted, twisting fury of proving that "you are right and they are wrong". Forgiveness on the other hand is still and quietly does nothing. It merely looks, waits and judges not.

It seems strange that by exerting no effort you can come to peace, by expecting nothing, you can gain it all. If you must be right, or better than, or more than someone else, you will not be at peace! These competitive attitudes usually stir up controversy. As Alfred Lord Tennyson said, "There is no joy but calm".

You understand that you are healed

when you give healing.

A Course In Miracles

8.   "Admit To Weaknesses"

There are many times when you can't do it yourselves, when you need others to show you the way. You may feel a little awkward about admitting your weaknesses. You shouldn't!

It may be that someone close to you can't bear to see you in a weakened state. It becomes their problem when they need you to be what they want rather than what you are. Since no one is perfect, and you can't be what others want you to be, that kind of relating can be shallow and dangerous. You need to be able to admit when you are weak, when you are wrong, and when you are frightened and still be assured that you are loved.

<u>A Course In Miracles</u> teaches us that we are always "perfect" in the spiritual sense. You are God's child, created of Love Itself and your identity can't be altered. Inside of you is your spirit, your soul, your inner being or child - it doesn't matter what you call it, it is there. Your divine essence never changes!

In a relationship, it is necessary to see the divine essence of another person, to know that their spiritual self does not change. It is there as a gift from God just like your spirit is. They are also a child of God. Once you have internalized this truth, you can look at the weaknesses of others and not be threatened by them. You can forgive the weakness and let it drift into the past.

Be humble and gentle.
Be patient with each other,
making allowances for each other's
faults because of your love.
Ephesians 4:2

9. "Deal With Your Anger"

Anger is a healthy emotion - one that can prompt you into action, or alert you to problems within. It is therapeutic; it is necessary! Untamed anger, however, may destroy relationships.

Problems arise when anger is not claimed, and hangs around for days, months, or years. Do you give yourself permission to act out your anger? All relationships will be subject to an occasional quick expression of anger with a quick apology. Then comes the search within you for clues to the anger.

Allowing constant outburst after outburst of damaging, unclaimed anger will erode any relationship. Ultimately, if you wish to live in peace, you need to own your own anger and deal with it immediately.

In your anger do not sin."
Do not let the sun go down
while you are still angry.
Ephesians 4:26

10. "Find Out Where Your Anger Comes From."

Finding out where your anger comes from is essential to living a spiritual life. You don't want to hurt others with angry irrational responses. You don't really want to be out of control. Usually it takes an introspective self-questioning to get to the roots of your anger.

It could be previously experienced neglect of parents, cruelty of siblings, or some injustice you had been forced to live with that triggers this anger. This is a very important issue so set aside the time for this kind of introspection.

A strong spiritual presence may disarm others, stop arguments before they start, and solve relational problems. It shows your partner you are strong enough within yourself to avoid manipulation, accusations, guilt, resentment, and anger. Be vigilant about your part in all relating. Take your own inventory and focus on yourself first.

Everyone should be quick to listen,

slow to speak and slow to become angry.

James 1:19,20

11. "Detach With Love"

A codependent person is "one who has let another's behavior affect him or her, and is obsessed with controlling that person's behavior."

If you are controlling others, you need to find out why. You need to ask why your happiness is contingent on someone else? Perhaps you have unrealistic expectations of some relationships.

In truth, your identity is centered within your spirit. You are a child of God first and partners in relationships second. As long as you are in relationship with any other human being, you need to maintain your ability to detach with love.

When you detach your mind from what is troubling you, your problems often solve themselves. Or it may be that leaving them to God gives Him a chance to take a hand in your affairs.

Each day, detach with love from the life and responsibilities of those you love. Detach, not in anger, but in a healthy way so that those around you may grow in their own way. Detaching requires faith - in yourself, in God, in other people, and in the natural destiny of things in the world.

But the fruit of the spirit is ... self-control.
Galatians 5:22,23

12. "Build A Community Of Love"

You are a spiritual creature who can determine your own destiny through belief, decision and action. Yet, you may not always choose to live spiritually, particularly in your relationships with others.

While a personal relationship with God is the key to renewing your own spiritual life, God is also manifest in people. To live as a child of God is to see others as his children also. If you are a child of God, so are those around you. And as children of God, you need to see others as equals in God's love.

In fact, so much of what you are independently is what you are interdependently. In <u>Spirituality</u> and <u>Recovery</u>, Father Leo Booth comments that "Only when you feel good about yourselves, and good about yourselves in relationship with others, will you be able to understand what it means to be a child of God."

You cannot think of loving yourself without loving others, or forgiving yourself without forgiving others. No matter how others have wounded you (which ultimately stems from their own woundedness) you cannot hate them if you are holding them in your mind as children of God. Living spiritually is seeing how you are "at one" with all other children of God.

But the wisdom from above is first pure;

then peaceable, gentle, open to reason,

full of mercy and good fruits,

without uncertainty and insincerity.

James 3:17

13. "Share Your Gifts"

Living spiritually means sharing the gifts God has given you. If you are a child of God, you have a "divine spark", or special gift from God. Your gift may be as quiet as eyes that exude an inner peace or as loud as some greatly artistic voice.

Whatever your gifts, your called to share abundantly, not because you own them but because God has lent them to you so that you can unleash the power of God's love throughout the world.

At all times you need to be open to the "holy moments" that make up your existence, to those soul searching times that keep you in touch with the beautiful souls of other children of God. Through your relationships with others, you continue to discover your own loving energy, your spirituality, and your God.

It is one of the beautiful compensations
of this life that no one can sincerely
try to help another without helping himself.
Charles Dudley Warner

— *Notes* —

Notes

Spring _____ 28
  1. "You Are The Hero Of Your Life" _____ 30
  2. "God's Will For You Is Joy" _____ 31
  3. "Listen To Your Inner Voice" _____ 32
  4. "There Is An Infinite Abundance Of Love" _____ 33
  5. "Dedicate Your Life To God And Serve Others" _____ 34
  6. "Put First Things First" _____ 35
  7. "Keep It Simple" _____ 36
  8. "Forgiveness Is Your Primary Function' _____ 37
  9. "Find Peace By Forgiving Your Parents" _____ 38
  10. "Breathe, Step Back And Reflect" _____ 39
  11. "Find Time To Pray" _____ 40
  12. "Be Still And Know God" _____ 41
  13. "There Is Always A New Day -A Second Chance" _____ 42

Spring

The Spring Season

In the winter season there is a period of darkness. It can be a cold lifeless time. It's as if winter is the twilight hour, a time of closure. But there is always the hope of rebirth. Spring brings that rebirth!

It silently comes, bringing a time to prepare for newness. No great event in nature happens without transitions. Winter is by itself the miraculous transition from the abundance of the Fall to the "newness" of Spring.

At the end of Winter as the temperatures gradually become warmer, as the water from the snow runs off, as sunlit hours grow longer, the buds return to push up the moist soil. This is a promise of new abundance!

Spring is a gradual happening with its own interim days! In the early Spring we think about the marvels of renewal that surround us every day, seeing the balanced resonance of our relationship with all things. We see how we are always sustained as God's children, by his unending love. Times of transition can be hopeful, exciting days with wonder and anticipation, but they also can extract from us faith, endurance and patience.

These days are our "dim-lit" hours before the sunrise, our days of gradual enlightening. Let us rejoice in these days that God has made and be glad for them.

In early grief, at the death of a dearly beloved one, we go through the darkness of winter, suffering each painful loss, remembering the immediate warmth, the touch, the connection of a love that is gone. At first, that is all we feel, until slowly there is a transition to acceptance, gratitude and a renewed hope of love. Like the seasons, we transition from Winter to Spring.

Reflecting on the quiet transitions of Spring tells me God is always there. No matter how uncertain the future seems, all we need to do is recognize God's presence. We can reach out by making conscious contact through prayer.

In these interim days, God speaks to us with subtle messages letting us know a new season is coming-a burst of warmth, a spurt of growth, a shock of bright color that emerges out of the darkness of winter. Change brings new graces. Symbolically, like the stream of light that slowly rises on the ocean at sunrise or falls into the sea at sunset, we are always connected to the source of our light, to God.

But, even more importantly, God provides for us after the sun has set, in the remaining dim light, until the moon rises and connects us once again to its light. In the interim days of Spring, there may be silence, growth, vulnerability, and anticipation but always there is God.

We learn in all seasons "there is only God".

1. "You Are The Hero Of Your Life"

All transitions are steps of progress. Each day will bring something different as you progress to a new stage of growth. If we were to hurry spring along in the ending days of winter, we would kill all the growth. We cannot drive the growing process- just by its nature it needs transitional time.

So you need to accept your place in your own growing -your moment of progression. No, you can't "be there" -complete and perfectly enlightened at any moment of your life. Something is dying and something is being born within you.

So often you may rebel against the changing seasons of your life when the truth is you are merely being led to a new place. If you scream and kick along the way as each change occurs, you may never enjoy this moment.

You are free to hang onto today's problems for as long as you want to. God will not wrest them from your mind. It is up to you to decide when the time is right for release.

Look it cannot be seen- it is beyond form.
Listen, it cannot be heard - it is beyond sound.
Grasp, it cannot be held - it is intangible.
Tao Te Ching

2. "God's Will For You Is Joy"

All of us want to live joyfully, content with the world around us, without petty complaints, happy within. These are our goals. We can see joy in others, but how do we get it?

First, you need to recognize God's will for you is joy. It is inconceivable that a loving parent could want anything but joy for his or her children. So it must be with God. Some people believe in a punishing God, who hands down judgments to teach us lessons. Yet, for me, God is Love Itself and I am his child. The unhappiness I experience doesn't come from God but from an arbitrary material world.

So much of what you see in everyday living is from the wrong perspective, your human perspective. You see material loss, violence, death and suffering. Trying to understand worldly suffering can become overwhelming.

Perhaps we were never meant to understand; perhaps your human world is full of illusions, while the real world is spiritual, of God, of Love, Itself; perhaps the only permanent world is within your spiritual self - the part that makes us children of God.

It is so much simpler for me to accept God's will for me as joy and to leave the rest of the mysteries of the universe to the world of illusions. Then, the world seems to work in conjunction with me as I cooperate with it.

May the God of hope fill you

with all joy and peace in believing

Romans 15:13

3. "Listen To Your Inner Voice"

Rest in God's presence today. Go inside to find that Higher Power - the ever present Eternal Presence. It is within - in the heart of hearts you call home. Rest in God awhile and know that all else is uneventful, incidental in comparison.

God's love is permanent, a part of your very being, but it needs to be touched each day. God reaches out to you in miraculous ways and all you need do is be quiet enough to hear His voice. All you need do is to acknowledge God's presence - to listen to Him as He speaks to you. Then, in grace you see a light that covers the path before you.

Silence allows us to detach from the world of confusion around us. It allows us to be in relationship with God, to talk to Him, but most importantly to hear His voice

When you hear the voice of God within you, you are able to give away what you hear to others. You witness to the presence of God with your serenity, your spirituality and, most importantly, you are quiet enough to receive the love that flows through others to you.

Embrace God's grace! Faith works because when you put your will and life into God's care, your life miraculously changes for the better. When you are open to grace, God comes to you.

All men come to him who keeps the one,

for there lies rest and happiness and peace.

Tao Te Ching

4. "There Is An Infinite Abundance Of Love"

Sometimes when you believe there's a scarcity of love, you try to conserve it. You think there can never be enough. You look for security that you don't need.

Your ego will tell you that you are unprotected, unlovable, alone in a frightening world; that you are not OK and that there is no way to trust anyone.

Your ego will tell you to search for one special love relationship that will bring you happiness. Then, you take ownership of someone demanding that they fill you in with love. The ego tells you there is a scarcity of love, but in essence, it's all around us.

The truth is that God is Love and you are God's child, so there is always an infinite abundance of love. All you need do is access it. When you take it and give love back to the world, it multiplies and comes back to you.

Each day, try not to listen to the voice of your separate self, your ego, but to the loving voice of God.

Your task is not to seek for love,

but merely to seek and find all the

barriers within yourself that you have built against it.

ACIM

5. "Dedicate Your Life To God And Serve Others"

It is not enough to believe in God's power and do nothing. You must wish to serve, to spread the light and energy of Love throughout the world. Simply, you must turn your will and your life over to the care of God, as you understand Him. That means ultimate trust in God's will; that means acceptance that God's will for us is joy; that means acceptance that you are not in charge.

Paradoxically, you are responsible for every word, thought and action that you do; however, God is in charge of the overall results. God has the power but you work within His power! Your forgiveness, your faith in the power of Love casts out fear and brings peace.

Each day, remember not to take back your life in a non-constructive way, a way that allows you to be invested in your own material expectations. But, do God's will through right living and goodness, as you dedicate your life to God.

Through His power within us,

you are the workers of miracles

and the seedlings of a transformed humanity.

-Marianne Williamson

6. "Put First Things First"

Remember to put first things first. Think through each situation in your life and do "the next right thing". Become guided by love in all that you do. Recognize fear as the opposite of love.

When fear comes to you, turn to faith. Remember other fearful times and recognize that your faith in God pulled you from that overwhelming place. If you choose to let him, God will be there again.

It is easy to get caught up in doing everything "perfectly" and find yourself running out of "self". You need to understand that you can't be all things to all people, do everything perfectly, or give yourself entirely to another. There must be a balance in giving. Don't give your spirit away totally, or deplete another's spirit by "too much of a good thing". Balance is the key.

In a world that is uncertain, it is good to know that God can do for you things that you cannot do for yourself. When you remember to put God first, all other relationships will certainly fall into place. Prayer is the only antidote for a fearful situation.

First things first - give all things to God this day.

Test all things; hold fast what is good.
Thessalonians 5:21

7. "Keep It Simple"

Because we live in a complex multi-dimensional world where we are constantly bombarded with information, we need to simplify our lives. We have become over crowded, over indebted, and over stressed.

You can begin by speaking simply. There is no need to clutter your life with too much useless conversation. Next, you can think simply. By ridding your minds of all the things you can't change, you can lighten the load of worry that you carry around.

Finally, you can live simply. "A person's life does not consist in the abundance of his possessions"(Luke 12:15); yet, some people are owned by their possessions. You pile up material goods that you insure against theft or loss. You pile up your schedule with appointments when you really want some quiet time. You involve yourselves in the lives of others when they need to work out their own destiny. Living simply means getting rid of some of the baggage.

How can you make time for God when you are so busy with the world? How can you find serenity in the midst of so much complexity? Keep it simple! Get back to basics and get back to yourself.

Now we have received, not the spirit of the world, but the spirit who is from God, that we might know the things that have been freely given to us by God.
I Corinthians 2:12

8.   "Forgiveness Is Your Primary Function'

You can't come to God by any other means than love. If you have hatred in your heart, you cannot know God or yourself.

How can you hope to know your true nature as a child of God without love? God is Love, Itself! Love is your legacy and to know love is to know God. Fear, resentment, hatred will drive out faith, acceptance, and serenity. These opposites cannot be housed in the same place.

Therefore, forgiveness is your primary function in life. There are no choices when it comes to forgiveness - the die is cast. If you can't look upon others with love, you can't see yourselves in the light of God's forgiveness. Surely, there will be some unforgivable sin that you carry just like your brother's sin. You are the same as your brothers and sisters.

Some people mistake forgiveness for approval of some wrongdoing. It is not up to me to judge others as damned. I don't have to approve of what they do, but I cannot judge them. That is the job of a Higher Power!

A lack of forgiveness always suggests that "I am better" - that I could never be as evil as that person. How blind we are when we refuse to forgive. Today, let God be the love in which you forgive.

I am a little pencil in the hand of God
who is sending a love letter to the world.
Mother Theresa

9. "Find Peace By Forgiving Your Parents"

As Dr. Harold Bloomfield explains in <u>Making Peace With Your Parents</u>, "Many 'here-and-now' conflicts that people have with their spouses, bosses, partners, and children are in part emotional enactments of suppressed feeling stemming from incidents that happened when they were children".

If your relationship with your parents was, or still is, troubled, you need to drop your defenses, and your pain, to allow the healing process to happen. Ultimately, you can only find peace by forgiving your parents for not being perfect.

If your parent has died you might still be able to find resolution. First, make a list of all the things you resented about your parent. Be specific. Use creative visualization by imagining your parent hearing you state these resentments, acknowledging your pain, and accepting your feelings. Visualize you and your parents together covered with a warm, radiant light. Let this be the reconciliation of God's love.

Give yourself the gift of forgiveness. The reconciliation between you and your parent has already taken place in the mind and heart of God. It is only a matter of time until you catch up whether it be in this world or the next.

10. "Breathe, Step Back And Reflect"

Reflection! It doesn't cost anything, can't be seen or felt, but it's essential to the soul. Our lives go too fast - it is fast food restaurants, instant news broadcasts, service vendors, and rush hour traffic that propels us along. There's no time to think.

"How can I focus?" you might ask. There are so many decisions at work, in a relationship, in parenting - and you can't think. It never seems to occur to you to stop what you are doing, put down the load for awhile and go some place to reflect.

Before you start the day, go to a place of certainty and peace, to connect with God's love, to ask for God's help and to become centered in the power of God. Develop a catalogue of prayers or affirmations that calm you. Talk to God with an honest heart and put yourself in a peaceful place.

During the day, when things get out of focus, breathe, step back and go back to that place within - reconnecting with God again. Then, at night, before you sleep make a conscious effort to bring your mind back to that place of peace again. Your days may be hectic, but God is always there with you.

Start each day with meditation,
and each week will take care of itself.
And remember I am with you always,
to the end of the age."
Matt 28:20

11. "Find Time To Pray"

Are you troubled by what you see in the evening news? Does it concern you that you can't turn on the television without being bombarded with images of death and violence? And do you consider this the only reality?

The reality of the material world can never bring you peace. The newspaper or TV will not reveal God's truth to us. When you turn to these images you are committing psychic death. If you turn to them alone for your reality, you ultimately will despair.

Each day, remember that in filling your mind with the things of God, you will find peace. Through prayer, you will find the channel for the re-establishment of your mental power reclaiming its divine element.

As Marianne Williamson says in Illuminata, "you pray for the capacity to forgive, to see innocence in people and to surrender all things to God. You pray to enter the mystery, to remember now, to no longer forget."

Each day, don't be influenced by images of the world, rather find time to shut off the world and go back home to God. Pray.

To pray is to descend with the mind
into the heart, and there to stand
before the face of the Lord,
ever present, all seeing.
Theophan

12. "Be Still And Know God"

In a world that is dominated by "doing", by recreational activity, recreational vehicles, recreational pleasures, it is difficult to sell silence; however, silence is the highest level of prayer.

It is in that deep and profound silence that you allow yourself to be still and know Him. In that silence you are changed. You are calmed. You are brought to a place of light.

Silence allows us to detach from the world of confusion around us. It allows you to be in relationship with your God, to talk to Him, but most importantly to hear His voice. You pray that God might cleanse your minds. Like a bright white light that fills a dark room, He comes to us in prayerful silence. You need to be ready to see that light, to feel its calming effect and to know peace.

Each day, before you begin your busy schedule, before you read the newspaper or turn on the TV - give yourself the gift of silence.

In moments of silence, realize you are recontacting your source of awareness.

D. K. Chopra

13. "There Is Always A New Day - A Second Chance"

The wonder of nature is that it always provides a second chance. When I see a massive expanse of ocean, waves rushing into the shore, with each wave toppling over the other, repeating its own rhythm, singing its own singular song, I am reminded of second chances.

Surfers go into this ocean battling to catch waves as they crash into shore. They fall and get up again to catch the next wave. There is always a next wave!

That is the wonder of God - your second chances. If you start a day, or even a lifetime, and it seems to go wrong, you can begin again. You can turn your life and your will over to the care of God at any moment of the day. That is your option!

You can celebrate new beginnings because there is no moment when all is lost. Out of your pain comes a new understanding. A beneficent God renews you each day. That second chance, like the waves of the ocean, is always there for us to catch.

Footsteps in the sand

Quickly washed away: the seashore mind

365 Tao

Notes

Notes

Summer		47
1.	"Holy Relationships Are Possible"	49
2.	"True Love Is A Decision"	50
3.	"Find The Wonder In Relationships"	51
4.	"Work On Understanding Another's Point Of View"	52
5.	"Let Go Of Your Problems"	53
6.	"Don't Insist On Being Right. Be Happy!"	54
7.	"Honesty Is The Best Policy"	55
8.	"You Can Be A Messenger Of Love!"	56
9.	"Rejoice In Each New Day"	57
10.	"Rituals That Give Symbolic Meaning To Your Life"	58
11.	"You Are Not Alone"	59
12.	"Believe There Is Nothing To Fear"	60
13.	"Look For Self 'Within' Not Outside Of You"	61

Summer

The Summer Season

In the closing days of summer, all things come together as a glorious harvest, which is really the ultimate relationship. The seeds have been sown in the warm earth, taken its nourishment, soaked up the rain, sprouted and grown to fruition. Now we reap the rewards of this summer growth participating with all that is beautiful in nature. *This season we celebrate the oneness of all things as we relate to God, to ourselves and others.*

Your seasonal Daily Guidance for Summer will focus on relationship - the joining together to make one. So often we think of how the magazine rack at the supermarket depicts love relationship: "How to Stay Crazy-in Love", "How to Please Your Man", or "Ten Ways to Make Your Sexual Life Better" Modern magazines give only a limited view of the meaning of intimacy. There is so much more to love and relationship.

Our first and primary relationship is with God. If we nurture that relationship, we have the power and love necessary to know ourselves, and the power and love necessary to love ourselves, and others. God is the source and we are His children. Like the seeds that take nourishment from the earth and rain, our spirits grow in the love of God.

Secondly, we need to take time to be with ourselves - to look within, reflect, pray, meditate - join with God. So often in the rush of everyday life, we neglect to see "how we act with ourselves is how we act with the world". When my self talk is berating, belittling, and mean, I will transfer that attitude to someone else. I must love myself as I am today! Remembering always my place as God's child. Without this consistent personal relating to me, I can't feel good about presenting myself to you.

Our third relationship is with the world - all others. Not just that special someone we favor but the old woman in the supermarket, the taxi-cab driver, our co-workers, and the child who nearly runs us over with her bike. All people are our teachers and we are theirs.

Leo Tolstoy once said, "I now understand that my welfare is only possible if I acknowledge my unity with all people of the world without exception". Life is not lived in a vacuum but in the "Holy instants of connection" to God, to ourselves, and to others.

What a joyous thought - to think of all the opportunities we have to come together, to blend our energy, making it into one new and more powerful force! We are God's children! We are not solely of the body, but of the spirit! In that sense we are joined! We are one!

The human race is most like unto God when it is most one, for the principle of unity dwells in Him alone.

Dante

1. "Holy Relationships Are Possible"

In your union with others, there is a spiritual connection that underlies every experience of love. You can make this spiritual connection a part of your everyday life. You can build holy relationships.

A "holy relationship" is based on a deeply felt mutual respect with each person seen as a spirit-filled child of God rather than an impersonal object. An unholy relationship is based on differences with each one thinking the other has what he does not. A partner stays until they think there is nothing left to steal.

In a holy relationship one person does not take from the other trying to make themselves whole. Each one has looked within and seen no lack! They are spiritually whole. Martin Buber in his acclaimed work, "I" and "Thou", describes lovers who relate in a spiritual way like a candle lit with a fiery tongue of flame repeatedly separating and returning to one.

God is within all of us. When you relate to others, you need to remember this and to see the holiness of each person you meet. All have their own integrity, their own spirit, and their own individuality before God.

Each day, see with a new vision all people you encounter. See God in them, understand them as your brothers and sisters, as children of God!

The spiritually evolved individual is an

extraordinary loving individual,

and with his or her extraordinary love

comes extraordinary joy.

M. Scott Peck

2. "True Love Is A Decision"

By changing your perspective of yourself, by attaining a spiritual wholeness, you improve your chances of relating in a spiritual way by bringing that spiritual self to all relationships. Seeing yourself as a child of God, you may also see others as His children; but, what is even more important, you treat others as His children.

Intimate partnerships can become holy when both partners accept their spiritual place in the relationship. The first thing you need to do is to return to the basic honesty that was inherent in us as children.

You need to feel that you have permission to "ask questions when you don't know"; you need to start out with trust not distrust; you need to re-learn how to express your feelings and how to play; and you need to praise your partner when appropriate. A return to innocence is a return to spirituality.

Society may teach us to protect ourselves with lies or excuses, to hesitate to ask questions, not to trust anyone, but those are the ways of the world not of God.

True love is not a feeling
by which you are overwhelmed.
It is a thoughtful decision.
M. Scott Peck

3. "Find The Wonder In Relationships"

There are three things that show wonder in healthy relationships. The first comes in a sense of purposefulness, a lack of disquietude. That does not imply a lack of decision making or problem solving. However, when two people see themselves as children of God, they learn to live in peace.

The second quality of a wondrous relationship is the sense of an ever-changing pattern. Nothing stays the same. Issues and problems are dealt with and dissolved, only to be replaced by new ones; however, the love remains.

Call it steadfastness, commitment, marriage, a bond that girds the relationship with strength. The pattern changes but in an awesome way, the relationship stays as strong as ever, as love, itself.

The third element in a wondrous relationship is power. No union is more powerful than a healthy spiritual relationship. It has power to become, and the power to remain the same. It has the power to take on all that would destroy its union.

The two will become one flesh.

So they are no longer two, but one.

Mark 10:8

4.   "Work On Understanding Another's Point Of View"

So often we have a tendency to rush right in with advice to solve other people's problems when in reality the last thing they need is advice. They need to be understood. It takes time to diagnose some one's problem, so don't rush in.

Most people are more involved in trying to find a solution than in trying to understand the person. Most people compare that person's problem with their own experience and fail to listen with "empathy".

Listening with "empathy" means that you seek first to understand how they feel. You let the person know that you hear by repeating their words back to them. You mirror their feelings by saying what you see in their expressions. You help them understand themselves.

When I asked one of my high school students what spiritual message she would like me to write for her, she said, "understanding". For a teenager there is nothing worse than feeling misunderstood, that to know a parent, teacher, or friend, isn't listening to you. Ultimately teens can feel very isolated.

Many things can be accomplished in life. Some men and women efficiently run corporations handling millions of dollars each year, and some doctors perform delicate surgery each day; but when it comes to understanding others, they are baffled. Understanding others is the primary ingredient in relationships because as Pascal said, "The heart has its reasons which reason knows not of."

Seek first to understand,

then seek to be understood.

Steven Covey

5.   "Let Go Of Your Problems"

Whenever a perceived problem or sorrow consumes you, it may be because you feel inadequate to solve that problem or survive that loss. You have simply forgotten the power of God and His plan in your life.

Remember that of yourself you are powerless, that God can handle all the problems you harbor within. Pray and reach to God - turning your problems over to Him.

When you lose a loved one, you cannot see that this loss will be replaced by a new love, a deeper appreciation of love, a stronger bonding someplace else. You do not see that God might be pointing you in a different direction.

Open the door and wait for God to show you what is next. In every tragedy, in every winter of despair, there is a birthing, a new idea, a new love, a new moment of glory. You are being tested to recognize your humanness, to humbly ask God for the patience, and faith to endure this darkness.

Each day, know that life is cyclical

- out of each dark time comes new energy, new life!

Those who sow in tears will reap

with songs of joy.

He who goes out weeping, carrying seed to sow,

will return with songs of joy,

carrying sheaves with him.

Psalms 126: 5,6.

6. "Don't Insist On Being Right. Be Happy!"

God's will for you is joy! You may not like what is happening to you, but if you can accept life, "on life's terms," you can be joyful. If you do not try to change a situation that can't be changed; you will not insist on being right all the time. You will accept loss and return all people to God in good condition. Today, you will feel joy.

Perhaps it's a matter of forgiving yourself? If you can't see beyond your mistakes, you may never see your spiritual self, that is, the forgiven child of God. When you remember only your mistakes, you picture yourself as sinful, and cannot find that child of God within.

It is through your internalized conviction as a child of God that you can come to see "you am enough," in fact, "you are holy, God's chosen one."

Today, remember that in the light of God's inheritance as God's children and in the light of God's love, you are everything, you are whole, you are perfect, and you are enough!

Blessed are those who have learned to acclaim you,

who walk in the light of your presence,

O Lord. They rejoice in your name all day long,

they exact in your righteousness.

Psalms 89: 15,16.

7.   "Honesty Is The Best Policy"

What does it mean to be honest? Living congruently implies honesty. When nothing you say contradicts what you think or do - that is honesty! When no thought opposes another thought, no act belies your word, and no word lacks agreement with another, you are truly honest.

Honest people are not in conflict with themselves; therefore, it is impossible for them to be in conflict with anyone or anything. Through this lack of conflict comes peace of mind.

If I say I am a father, do I act as a father? If I say I am a worker, do I act as a good employee should? If I say I am a wife, do I act as a wife does? If I say I am a good citizen, do I carry out those duties?

Why do honest men succeed? Simply because they never do their will alone but choose the greater good. They choose in perfect honesty, as sure of their choice as of themselves. In this sense, honest men and women become examples to the rest of us; they become teachers of God.

Each day, strive for that complete

unity between word and action that leads

to perfect peace.

No legacy is so rich as honesty.

William Shakespeare

8. "You Can Be A Messenger Of Love!"

If I love myself as God's child, I will live a life of love - that is the only gift I need give anyone. Once you have established a primary relationship with your Creator and accepted your place in the universe as His child, you are ready for your life's work.

As God's child, you already have all you need. You are complete in your oneness with God; therefore, what you do for a living doesn't matter as much as how you execute that chosen career.

You are here to project God's message of love, not to operate a tractor-trailer truck, write a legal document, pave a road, cure a patient, or lecture to an audience. You are of Love itself, and your purpose is to love. You can bless the world when you use a surgeon's knife, teach the alphabet, serve someone a bowl of soup, or scrub a floor.

Each day, become a messenger in your work and project a message of love - not one of fear, hatred, or resentment. You will understand when others cry out for love, and you will give love. When you turn your life and your will over to God, you're making a decision to go with the loving purpose of God.

It's not always necessary that you understand the direction of your life, but it is essential that you establish its loving purpose. No matter what your earthly job may be, live your life in love today.

Each one should retain the place in life

that the Lord assigned to him

and to which God has called him.

I Corinthians 7:17

9. "Rejoice In Each New Day"

Sometimes it's hard to be happy each new day- to rejoice and be glad in it. What about all the things you need to do this week? What about a sick child? What about all the things you worry about? What about that person who bothers us? It's the job, the bills, the responsibilities!

But when your perspective is right, when you understand that God's will for us is joy, it is much easier to be happy at the beginning of the day. Often, I think of past days and realize that the God who took care of me then is taking care of me now. The only time in my life when I was truly unhappy was when I refused to accept some part of my life and rebelled against those things that I couldn't change.

Each day, pray "God grant me the serenity to accept the things I cannot change, the courage to change the things I can, and the wisdom to know the difference."

This is the day the Lord has made;

let us rejoice and be glad in it.

Psalm 118 1:24

10. "Rituals That Give Symbolic Meaning To Your Life"

Ceremony, music, symbolic gestures, and objects usually mark the milestones in your relationships. For a deeper kind of relating, you need pay attention to the habits of ritual in your everyday life.

In your relationship with God, you need rituals of prayer. It need not be formal yet it should be a "conscious" contact. Sharing your life with God through prayer gives it a continuity that can't be equaled.

Marianne Williamson states in Illuminata "rites of passage are words that take us beyond words." All relationships need to be marked with ritual.

Whether it is an intimate relationship that marks its beginning with an anniversary, or a private ritual when you go to a special place, like your birthplace, to commemorate some event in your spiritual growth, or the act of going to the gravesite of a loved one. You need ceremony to give symbolic meaning to life, but most of all you need to reconnect with God in rituals of private prayer.

Each day, seek to understand the symbolic nature of all that you do; honor all the events of your life.

Ceremonies of light...

rites of passage...

rituals...

remind us of our oneness and

form society's connective tissue.

Marianne Williamson

11. "You Are Not Alone"

Once, I had an eighteen year old student of mine say to me, "What does it all mean? What's the meaning of life? That is all I want to know?" He confessed to being plagued with thoughts of suicide and was struggling with addiction. For him, life had no meaning because he saw himself disconnected from others - alone in an insane world!

The irony is no one can answer the question posed by my student. You must look within and fill the void by accepting your place in the pattern of all living things.

You can fill that spiritual void by remembering you are never alone. You are connected to the power and majesty of the universe; you are part of all life; you are of God.

Many of the astronauts have described being in space as a spiritual experience. It is easy to understand why. You cannot look at the majesty of the universe without being drawn to God. "Nothing comes from nothing" - so it is within the great order and process of the universe that a Higher Power becomes evident. It must be even more evident when you are in the outer stratospheres.

And you are connected to the entire universe - you are a living part of the whole. It's only when you see yourselves as disconnected from the energy of God, the power and majesty of all He has created, that you feel desolate and alone.

And you know in all things God works together

for the good of those who love him,

who have been called according to his purpose

Romans 8:28

12. "Believe There Is Nothing To Fear"

At certain times in my life, I became filled with a sense of fear. It would catch me up into itself dominating my thinking, pulling me into a downward spiral until I couldn't think straight. My friends tried to reassure me with varying degrees of success.

Then, a spiritual man told me that he had found a solution to the problem. He told me that the only way to overcome fear is through faith. He said he began to get up early in the morning and read his meditations for the day. These prayerful readings calmed him and replaced his fear with faith.

Today I do the same. Whenever I sense any fearful response, I know I must go back to God to find my serenity. A calm comes over me as soon as I read of God's love because I know that I am safe in God's loving care. That is how this book of Reflections came to be!

"The awareness that there is nothing to fear shows that someplace in your mind, though not necessarily in a place you recognize as yet, you have remembered God, and let his strength take the place of your weakness. The instant you are willing to do this there is indeed nothing to fear". ACIM Lesson 48.

There is no fear in love,

but perfect love casts out fear.

I John 4:18

13. "Look For Self 'Within' Not Outside Of You"

Do you sometimes think you are not enough? Not good enough? Not smart enough? Not attractive enough? If you have a vague sense of not being "enough", you are not alone.

Many psychological difficulties- anxiety, under achievement in school, emotional immaturity, sexual dysfunction, chronic spells of depression, - can be attributed to low self-esteem. Many people suffer from insecurity, self-doubt, and guilt, becoming afraid to participate fully in life.

Usually thinking you are not enough is a spiritual issue. It disavows the existence of the spiritual self and indicates you are relying on your human powers alone, not the power and presence of God. Thinking you are not enough indicates a lack of faith and a misunderstanding of your true nature a child of God.

No matter where you are in life, no matter what is happening, you are always doing the best you can with the knowledge and awareness you have. You are perfect just the way you are. There is no timetable and you can't progress too slowly or too quickly. Even with your imperfections, you are spiritually perfect as a child of God.

The heart is the hub of all sacred places.

Go there and roam.

Bhagawan Nityanada

Notes

Notes

Autumn	66
1. "Remember God's Love Is Permanent"	68
2. "A Kind Word Can Change A Life"	69
3. "Listen With Your Heart"	70
4. "Your Spiritual Job Is Your Most Important One"	71
5. "Fear Drives Out Faith"	72
6. "Make Peace Your Goal"	73
7. "No One Can Make You Happy But Yourself"	74
8. "Avoid All Extremes"	75
9. "To Give Is To Receive"	76
10. "Honor The Sacred Nature Of Relationship"	77
11. "Your Thoughts Can Heal Or Harm Others"	78
12. "When One Door Closes Another Opens"	79
13. "The Journey Is The Final Answer"	80

Autumn

The Fall Season

As the summer reaches its fullness, the sun warms us, plants and flowers burst into bloom, and we are reminded of the generosity of nature. We are reminded of God's goodness. *The Fall season centers on the idea of abundance!*

Yet, even with all this bounty before us, there are times when we fail to see it. We can become lost in our own perception of "scarcity". We think there is not enough love, money, sex, prestige, or not enough appreciation of us. It is this lack of something that we dwell on.

How do you look at your life? Do you see the abundance of it? Do you look at your children, hear them laugh out loud, and see their health? Do you appreciate your sight as you read this page? Are you thankful for the food you buy at the supermarket? Can you move without pain? Does someone love you? Are you hopeful, peaceful and happy? Can you see the great gifts you have?

Most of life's problems come out of a place of spiritual impoverishment. We are unable to feel "soul satisfied" and want more. We try to fill the hole in our soul with many things: money, pills, alcohol, food, any number of things. But, in reality, our souls respond to faith, love, grace, hope, and forgiveness. When we discover these gifts, we are free to experience peace and joy.

As Seneca said, "Unhappy is the man, though he rule the world, who doesn't consider himself supremely blessed". In this season, let us concentrate on those things which come to us freely: grace, peace, forgiveness, understanding, love and joy.

We can celebrate our roles as children of God understanding this is our most essential role in life. Whenever we need strength and love, it's there through our connection to God; never to be denied us, never to fail us. We are sustained by the love of God, we are his children.

Reading seasonal daily meditations reminds us of our place in the world, of our connection to God and others. It also reminds us of how much we have to be thankful for rather than letting us become preoccupied with how little there is.

Whenever I am faced with a difficult time, I go immediately to spiritual readings. By letting the words wash over me, I begin to feel a sense of well being. Often, I repeat the reading and sometimes I take a thought with me carrying it within my mind as I face each new decision that day. For example, I say to myself, "God is the Love in which I live". These words comfort; they empower me!

May the words here provide seasonal daily guidance to you ever bringing you back to a recognition of the abundance of God's gifts.

1.   "Remember God's Love Is Permanent"

There are some days when my whole being seems cloudy and overcast. It's as if there is no sunshine anywhere. Those are the days I especially need to turn to God. I can easily take charge of my own life when all I need to do is to remember that I am sustained by the love of God.

No matter what problems confront you today or tomorrow, you are sustained by the Love of God. You may think trivial things sustain you: like money, pills, clothing, influence, prestige, being liked, and knowing the right people. All these things are replacements for the Love of God. They sustain the ego and let us identify with our bodies rather than our spirit.

Only the Love of God will protect you in all circumstances. It will lift you out of every trial, and raise you high above all perceived dangers of this world into a climate of perfect peace and safety. It will transport you into a state of mind that nothing can threaten, nothing can disturb, and where nothing can intrude upon your internal calm.

God's love is permanent - a part of your very being but God needs to be accessed every day. He reaches out to us in so many miraculous ways and all we need to do is to be available to hear His voice.

I am sustained by the Love of God

A Course In Miracles: Lesson 50

2.　"A Kind Word Can Change A Life"

Sometimes you forget that your greatest gift is the very moment you are living in. You lose the present to the past or future.

"Living in the moment" can mean giving a child who stutters time to speak, or listening to a friend's concern about her husband's health - and being grateful to know that child, or have that friend. Through your attention, you can give others the gift of love.

Through your affirming words, you can contribute a positive message to someone, which may return to them from time to time when they have lost confidence, or are afraid. Perhaps your words will shape future actions. But the moment to speak is now!

Words are powerful because they can influence us. They can be instruments of spiritual growth or destruction; they can project love or fear. Not only can words shame a soul, pierce a mind, or uplift a heart in a few seconds, but also, they can stay with you for a lifetime. You remember what others say. You remember words.

God works through you using not only your actions but also your words. Each day, speak in a way that teaches only love.

A gentle answer turns away wrath,

but a harsh word stirs up anger.

Proverbs 22: 24:25

3.   "Listen With Your Heart"

Love can hear all kinds of things; love can see things differently. Do you listen in a loving way? Listening with your heart instead of your ears is essential to the success of relationships. Listening is an empathetic response. Not only does it internalize what it hears and sees, but it interprets that information with the understanding that you either "give love", or make a desperate "cry for love."

When someone close turns away to search for love someplace else - think what an act of desperation that must be. Think of what degree of "aloneness" drove them to that place. To move away from a previously loving relationship can be a "cry for love".

Listen with your heart when you see someone trying to stir up jealousy, when you see anger, or rebelliousness. Think of the desperate place those actions and emotions come from.

Reacting to an obvious "cry for love" with a refusal to love will only generate more self-effacing destructive behavior. Acting in a loving way might produce the opposite effect: it might stop the destruction.

Live in harmony with one another.

Romans 12:16

4. "Your Spiritual Job Is Your Most Important One"

"What do you do?" people say to one another, and the answer is, "I teach", "I'm a janitor", "I'm an accountant". We often define ourselves by the roles we play in life yet we seldom think of ourselves as the image and likeness of God. Yet, we are His children and that is our primary role in life!

What will you do this day as God's child? Will you treat someone with kindness? Will you forgive someone? Will you live in love today? Or will you designate all your time to your earthly role of being the teacher, the janitor, or the accountant? How much more significant is your spiritual job?

As you go through the adventure of this day, will you take time to talk to your Father, Mother, Divine Essence, Your Higher Power, praising that One by saying "I love you, my God"? Then to hear the answer coming back from the center of your being, "I love you too my child".

Remember you can rely on God to solve all your problems, that your spiritual role in life is your most important job.

We alone must make something of yourselves,

Transforming ourselves into instruments for experiencing the deepest spiritual essence of life.

Tao Te Ching

5. "Fear Drives Out Faith"

When we trust in our own strength, we have every reason to be apprehensive, anxious and fearful. What can we protect or control? What is there in us that gives us the ability to be aware of all the facets of any problem, and to resolve them in such a way that only good can come out of it? What is there in us that gives us the recognition of the right solution and the guarantee it will be accomplished?

Of yourself, you can do none of these things. To put your faith in yourself alone without God is to put your faith in weakness. To put your faith in yourself with God is to put your faith in strength. "The strength of God in you is successful in all things." (ACIM).

Today, reach past your own weakness to the source of all strength. Search for the situations in your life in which you have invested with fear, and move past that fear by telling yourself that "God is the strength in which I trust"(ACIM: Lesson 47).

This message is the answer to whatever confronts you today. Through the Love of God within you, you can resolve all seeming difficulties without effort and insure confidence.

(ACIM Lesson 50)

6. "Make Peace Your Goal"

There are so many distractions to your peacefulness. It's the workplace, or home problems, your need to seek perfection, or to do things like everyone else. Do you sometimes allow the distractions of the world greater priority than these things deserve?

There is within you a place of surety, a place where you can get back to God. It's up to you to go to that place in prayer and meditation - to push away the world for a few minutes each day. Spiritual peace is your primary goal.

To be in "sync" with God is to be at peace. It isn't necessary to be right all the time, to be rich, or richer, or to be acclaimed but it is necessary to find peace.

Ovid said, "There is a God within us, and we glow when he stirs us" and Plato said, "the body is the tomb of the soul". Today, be mindful, less of the body and more of the soul. Look to your spiritual self and find peace and love.

When we are unable to find

tranquility within yourselves,

it is useless to seek it elsewhere.

Rochefoucauld

7.   "No One Can Make You Happy But Yourself"

You have an inner voice that leads you to truth and love. All you have to do is to find that voice within. Once fear and hatred are dispelled, you will be free to love. Positive affirmations remind you of who you are and help you to project positive messages to others. Changing your thinking changes your life. Let your gentle, loving inner voice change you from the inside out.

Whenever negative self-talk comes in, you have a choice. You can listen to these outdated messages, or you can shape positive new ones. It takes reprogramming! Because our minds are like a computer, they take in everything - the good and the bad. Messages are filed away and brought up at will. All of what you have heard in the past is saved; however, you have the power to sort or delete messages; you have the power to control your mind.

Your happiness requires that you responsibly take charge of your self-talk. Because negative self-talk can lead to negative behaviors and positive self-talk can lead to positive behaviors, you control the course of your life by your thinking. God's will for you is joy, but you must be willing to open your mind to positive messages.

Happiness depends on yourselves
Aristotle

8. "Avoid All Extremes"

You sometimes bring excesses to your life: loving too much, entertaining too much sadness, allowing too much fear - just too much of anything.

God never meant us to be involved in extremes. His beneficent love takes care of us providing a perfect balance in all things. How can you doubt when you see the universe which is so perfectly in harmony?

When you lose control of your emotions and become excessively angry, you are giving in to your emotions. When you think in "black and white" terms, you lose sight of the goodness and greatness of God. He will provide for any scarcity in any situation. When it becomes dark, he will bring light.

It is the light of peace that will surround you this day; it is the love of God that will sustain you. Look within today!

Each day, find that gentle,

balance in your feelings and your thoughts.

To everything there is a season and

a time to every purpose under heaven.

Ecclesiastes 3:1

9. "To Give Is To Receive"

Sometimes you need to hear yourself speak the message so that you fully understand it yourselves. Sometimes you do not recognize what you have until you give it away. Real giving is not of material possessions but of forgiveness and love. If I love myself as God's child, I will live a life of love - that is the only gift I need give anyone.

Do you ever think, "What is my purpose? Why am I here? Well, when you are in close relationship with God, you become His messengers. You perform your part by first accepting His message for yourself; then, you show you understand it by giving it away. You give to receive!

The concept of "giving and receiving being one" is mysterious to me. But I do know that whenever I extend light or energy in a positive way, it comes back to me. There are no exceptions to these miracles. They just keep happening!

No one can receive and understand
he has received until he gives.
For in the giving is his own acceptance
of what he has received.
ACIM Workbook page 154

10. "Honor The Sacred Nature Of Relationship"

When you are in relationship with a loved one, you need to "hold them sacred". Some people join in an intimate relationship to gain wealth, to have children, or for social or sexual reasons. These are the world's reasons for joining, but the spiritual purpose for an intimate union is that each partner might grow spiritually.

If you contribute to the spiritual deterioration of the one you love then you do not love them, you are using them to bring harm unto themselves. That is not a holy joining together but an unhealthy partnership.

When you "hold each other sacred", you understand the need to set and maintain boundaries. As with all that is sacred, there are limits that need to be honored.

You would not bring profanities to church, yet you sometimes may hurl them at your partner. There is nothing more sacred than the soul of another human; nevertheless, you allow a soul to be defiled.

Each day, honor the sacred nature of all people but especially those you love.

Genuine love is self-replenishing.
The more I nurture the spiritual growth of others,
the more my own spiritual growth is nurtured.
M. Scott Peck

11. "Your Thoughts Can Heal Or Harm Others"

Your thoughts can be powerful! There are courses on mind control, books about mind-body connection and many new alternative medical procedures that stress the power of thought.

<u>A Course In Miracles</u> teaches that there is no such thing as a neutral thought. If you think angry, negative things about others they will receive those messages even though you never utter a word aloud. So, you need to remember that you are sending energy to others with your thoughts.

If you wish to pray for others, send positive loving energy in their direction and they will receive it. If a family member is having a difficult meeting at a certain hour, send loving energy to fortify him/her. It works!

Why should you think you could only contact another through the body? The mind has its own power, its own energy. If there are people no longer in your life, send some energy in their direction. If someone has harmed you, rather than becoming flooded with resentment, send loving energy to him or her. Perhaps a miracle will happen; perhaps they will come to understand how they have harmed you. There is nothing as powerful as the energy of love.

Have your minds ready for action.
Keep alert and set your hope
completely on the blessing
which will be given.
Peter 1:13

12. "When One Door Closes Another Opens"

Sometimes when a year ends, we look longingly back at the one before, or ahead apprehensively to the one coming. Yet, we are told that each season has its charm, and its purpose under heaven.

It is wise not to spend too much time looking at the closed door so as not to miss the opportunity, which is opening before you. Endings are a part of life and have their place. Celebrate your endings by anticipating the joy of a new season.

Nature is reflective of life mirroring your endings and beginnings. You leave a marriage, your youngest son goes off to college, you retire after thirty years, or your vacation comes to an end. In every phase of your development, you must recognize endings.

There is always a sadness that accompanies transitions but with each ending comes a new beginning. Look to see the new door that has opened before you!

God took care of you in this phase of your life and will be there in the new beginnings. You need not be afraid of a new season rather you need you welcome it.

When one door of happiness closes, another opens,

but often you look so long at the closed door,

you do not see the one which has opened for us.

Helen Keller

13. "The Journey Is The Final Answer"

Sometimes you may feel like you are living in a vacuum - that you are stagnant. Yet, no day leaves you just as you were yesterday. There will be something new about you tonight as you retire and even something new as you awake from your dreams.

Today, honor your past year, remembering it with pride. Celebrate what motivated you to come to this place. Drawing from the past and present, you can look forward to the future.

Perhaps it is something you are learning that will prepare you to give more to the world; perhaps some work that will bring love or service to others. Perhaps this day you are becoming closer to God with a new spiritual awareness filling your spirit.

Whatever it is, you will never stagnate, or live in a vacuum, you are always <u>becoming</u> - like all things in nature! Heraclitus said, "Nothing is permanent but change". Each moment you are changing - growing, healing, losing, gaining, slowing down, or speeding up. It is just the way it is!

You are constantly becoming

Honor all that you have been, all

that you are, all that you will be.

Lisa Engelhardt

Notes

Notes

Also by Christine A. Adams

Spirituality: A Life Force

ABC's of Grief – A Handbook for Survivors

Let Go and Let God

Teacher of God

Holy Relationships

Living in Love

September Love

Claiming Your Own Life

School Factory

Love, Infidelity, and Sexual Addiction

Gratitude Therapy

One Day At A Time

Learning To Be A Good Friend

Happy To Be Me

Worry, Worry, Go Away

God Made Us One By One

Watch for more at her website

http://www.christineaadams.com/

Did you love *Seasons*? Then you should read

Here is a sample of her latest book,

"Spirituality: A Life Force"

SPIRITUALITY:
A LIFE FORCE

CHRISTINE A ADAMS

Chapter One: Spiritual Teaching

A special teacher--everyone seems to have a "special teacher" story! My story started in the seventh grade with Mrs. Parsons, the most loving teacher I ever had. Ironically, I remember her being especially well dressed.

I wondered how she got everything to match so <u>well</u>? Or is it <u>good</u>? "Well" and "good." She told us something about those words. Well, anyway her shoes and her belt match, and it's just the right color to go with her beige skirt and sweater. She's matched up like that, not just once a week, but every day. Today she's sitting on the radiator by the window watching us finish our test.

Diagramming sentences. It's getting so hard. I think this sentence has double or triple gerund phrases. Oh! Oh! Here she comes!

"When you finish, Christine. You and your cast can go out in the hall to rehearse."

"Alright, Mrs. Parsons."

I loved the idea of having my own cast of players, so I put down three parallel lines and joined them with a dotted line, put my paper on the desk and gave the signal to Jimmy and Peggy.

This week we would do a crazy play called "Who Put The Overalls In Mrs. Murphy's Chowder?" It was based on a song that came straight from Ireland just like my mother, Bridget McKenna. I hope these kids get it! "It" being Irish and all.

Everyone laughed when we were running around the front of the room trying to find out who put the pants in the soup--so I guess the play was a success. Mrs. Parson's stopped laughing long enough to say something about "unusual and different." She always said something nice!

Just then the bell rang. In their rush to get out, some of the kids knocked over the pot and the big spoon we were using for props. Mrs. Parsons helped us pick up the stuff. I told her some of my ideas for next week and she said, "That seems like a good idea, Christine. Why don't you write it up and I'll look at it."

And I've been writing things up ever since. Thirteen books printed in 24 countries and as many languages. And some place out there in the world there's 2,000,000 separate non-fiction pieces in print that happen to have my name on them. It all began when she said, "Christine, why don't you write it up?"

But we did a lot more than silly little plays those years. I was fortunate enough to get Mrs. Parsons for English for three years. They moved her up and somehow, she kept getting our class. She made sure I understood the "well" and "good" thing, diagrammed more tough sentences, and studied Shakespeare's **Merchant of Venice.**

Mrs. Parsons had this kind of tricky learning. You got a "contract" and decided how much work you would do and what your grade would be. Everyone would try to get an A and we all put together this Globe theatre thing. But we learned!

I learned so much in those years that English became my favorite subject in high school, I majored in English in College, and got my Master's in British Literature. Then, I went right out in the world and taught British Literature to high school seniors for 32 years. Just like Mrs. Parsons, the same old thing, diagramming sentences, Shakespeare, and contracts! Some of my students even became English teachers like me.

But there's more than English to the Mrs. Parson's story. There was something about the way she cared for everyone. Her sense of fairness was just like her matching outfits--the same all the way around. It didn't matter if life was hard for you, or if you were poor, she loved you just the way you were. Simply put, she had a way of loving and valuing you until you could love yourself. She did it by teaching you what she was and what you were to her!

She was awfully busy in those days loving and caring for so many kids. It was like they were her own huge family and she wanted them to make it in the world. She set a high standard for herself and for us. We noticed! We listened!

During my freshman year, which was my last year with Mrs. Parson's, my father died, and my mother was left with eight kids from ages two to fifteen. We didn't hear many Irish songs around our house anymore. But Mrs. Parsons helped me find my way through that painful year. Then, she continued to help my brothers and sisters as they came along. These were discouraging times, but she always cared and held us to a high standard. Again, simply put, she loved and valued us until we could love ourselves.

One thing about Mrs. Parsons, she was tough. She never gave up on us. We all tested her, each one of us in a new and different way. Sometimes she was the last ally on the playing field.

We're all a little older these days. Now, I can call Mrs. Parsons, "Jenny". She is still my inspiration, my teacher, and my friend. Some days we talk about teaching English with an excitement that only two former English teachers can muster up. We talk about how great it was to be a teacher, and tell stories about "our school kids." Some days we talk of memories of my youth, or her youth. Some days we just talk about life. But we never run out of things to talk about.

And when I tell her I have an idea for a new book, she keeps saying to me, "Christine, why don't you write that up?" And I do. Things haven't changed much really. I still love and admire her now just as I did then. Sometimes I remember the day the class laughed about the overalls in Mrs. Murphy's chowder and the tone of her voice when she said, "unusual and different." And I think how strange it is that I remember the tone of her voice?

When I think of her tone of voice, I remember to tell her, "You are the reason my life began to take form--back in the seventh grade, and continues moving forward today. You were my best teacher!"

But what is a good teacher?

In the eyes of the world we think of good teachers as the ones who give special information to "learners." That special learning might be an area of the teacher's expertise: math, language arts, physics, science--areas of expertise that pertain to a body of knowledge within the physical world. In that sense and on those occasions, the teacher does impart special information to the learner.

Yet almost everyone has a Mrs. Parsons story like mine. A story of someone who reached beyond the body of knowledge in some spiritual way. The teaching might not have occurred in a classroom setting. The teacher might have been a family member, a friend or even a stranger.

It was someone who provided an inspiring example to the learner; someone who believed in themselves first and then transferred that belief to the student and encouraged them. That is really why these teachers are remembered--not for the grammar, the equations, the formulas they taught or situations of life they shared with you. They are remembered for the love they showed.

When love and caring are involved, a new kind of teacher emerges, and the lesson is spiritual. The student learns to love by the example of love given. These teachers become spiritual teachers of love, or "Teachers of God."

Of course, I followed in Mrs. Parson's footsteps and became an English teacher. I tried to live up to her example and the learner became the teacher--literally. In following a teaching profession, I had plenty of opportunities to show love for my students and many times my students, the learners, became my teacher.

Each year as I started my school year, inevitably, there would be a boy or girl who was so starved for love that they became a discipline problem to get attention. They would be abusive in language, loud, and unruly; therefore, they became the first to report to the principal's office.

I remember Billy, a tall good looking senior, who appeared to be tough and mean. Billy had disruption down to a science! There were interruptions, burping in class, side comments and faces in his repertoire. I complied with his wishes for attention and sent him directly to the principal's office.

On the third trip, he divulged this information as he left the room, "Just trying to break my record. Last year's English teacher threw me out thirty-three times." I thought about that and decided to stop throwing him out. I began "to teach only love."

When he was abusive, I went up to him and in a loving voice corrected him. He didn't know what to do with the love. This might have been the first time anyone treated him that way.

As the year progressed, the situation got better when Billy was allowed to read Stephen King in an independent reading program. He devoured the books and remained quiet in class. When I went to The American Bookseller's Convention that year, I told Stephen King's publisher about Billy and he sent copies of his latest books. Billy was impressed!

The turning point came when I did a positive affirmations exercise with the class. Each student was supposed to list ten positive things about another student. No one picked Billy! So, I made up his list!

He watched me write: 1. tall 2. good-looking 3. nice smile 4. dark hair 5. loyal 6. persistent 7. loves to read 8. beautiful face 9. dark eyes 10. never forgets. When I was done, he smiled and said, "How did you know that stuff." I said, "I just know, Billy." Teaching is not all English-- it's love.

It was true Billy was a terrible student--ill disciplined, aggravating, rude, and disrespectful. But I asked God to let me see him differently through the eyes of love rather than fear. By changing my perspective of him, I changed his of himself. It's like that--love generates love.

We give love to others so that we can remain at peace within ourselves. I didn't let Billy run rampant over the class as we did the typical test of authority in the early days of the class. Then, when it was appropriate, I switched and let love in--not out of weakness but out of strength. There's the difference. So many people think it's weak to be defenseless but, at appropriate times, defenselessness shows great power. Teaching love looks passive sometimes, but it generates a lasting energy.

A child of God is a "teacher of God."

I first encountered the term, "A Teacher of God", in reading **A Course In Miracles**. Before that time, I believed that Sister Theresa, Gandhi, or the Dali Lama might fit that description but not the ordinary person.

Then, as I continued to read **The Course** and write about love in **Living In Love**, published in 1993 by Health Communications, Inc., I began to understand that we all are teachers. Whether we know it or not, we all teach what we are. If we believe that God is Love, and that we are of God; then we teach only Love. In that spiritual sense we are "Teachers of God."

The teacher and learner are the same!

Another concept that baffled me at first was the notion that the teacher and learner are the same. How could that be? I always saw the teacher as the leader imparting some special information to the learner--using the worldly definition of teaching. However, as we learn, we teach by showing what we are.

Let's look at teaching as a demonstration. **The Course** describes two thought systems: one governed by the ego and the material world of illusions and the other governed by the spirit. It makes sense that if you choose the spiritual path, you will teach what you are learning, as a matter of fact; you will witness to attest what you believe. In that sense the teacher and the learner are the same.

"In this sense spiritual teaching is not done by words alone. It is done through every situation of your life which becomes a chance to teach others what you are and what they are to you. No more than that, but never less!" (ACIM)

Examples of spiritual teaching!

Parenting affords us the opportunity to teach what we are and to demonstrate to our children what they are to us. The world can be falling down around the child but as long as there are parental examples of love and courage, the learning is going on.

In recounting my childhood in an unpublished autobiographical work entitled **The Chokecherry Tree,** I wrote of a time of great significance--the end of World War 11. As important as the war was in my memory, even more significant was the night of the birth of my brother, David.

1945 -- The End of World War 11-- and the Birth of David

Then it happened! President Franklin Delano Roosevelt died. I guess he hadn't been well for quite a while. A man named Harry Truman became president. People worried about the war effort and what would happen in America. Everyone was very sad when F.D.R. died. It was like the whole world turned dark overnight.

Suddenly, a short time later, that darkness lifted when the war ended in 1945. There were stories about people dancing in the streets, and newspaper pictures of soldiers and sailors kissing girls. Everything seemed brand new. Shining--like the buttons on the soldiers uniforms.

Bridie McKenna, my mother, was due to have a new child. On the night, the sixth child, David, was born, it snowed. The whiteness began to collect on the windows in the kitchen. The driveway filled up, the front porch steps were slippery.

When Mike came home from work, he realized they were in for a terrible nor'easter, so he shoveled out the driveway before supper. "I've had a little pain, off and on," she said as they sat down to supper. The corn beef and cabbage was piled in a dish in the middle of the table. Steam rose into the air. The butter was on a long narrow dish beside the bread.

Mike knew it might be a long night, so he ate heartily. The kids ran around the kitchen table playing together. "Mommy, Michael is hitting us," the girls reported to their weary mother.

"Mike" she answered directing the question to her weary husband. Mike reluctantly left his food and went into the living room to straighten out the kids. He put Danny in his playpen, gave Michael a puzzle and Raymond some trucks to play with and sent the girls to their rooms to do their homework.

"Michael you keep an eye on Raymond and Danny, and have that puzzle done by the time I come back," he said sternly to his son. A break in the noise ensued. There was a secret kind of signal that came over the house when their father "straightened out the kids". They all knew this was no time to disobey.

"What if I have to go tonight," she said touching her stomach.

"We'll make it. I'll put the chains on now so as to be ready. We'll put the kids down in their clothes and dress them warm, pack em and go. Don't ye worry, Bridie. When it's time. We'll make it!"

Bridie always went to Wyman's Maternity home in Kittery to have the babies. There she would meet Doctor Shapleigh who delivered all the McKenna's. Tonight, she was worried about the seven mile ride to Kittery.

Later that night, Bridie's water broke, and she woke Mike to tell him it would be "soon". No one quite knew what "soon" meant but it did mean you'd better find your boots and mittens and put them on as fast as you can, and then find your brothers boots and mittens and pull them over their hands and feet as quick as you can.

The snow swirled around the car and the windshield wipers beat at the windows. It was like being in a tunnel where there was no end just white swirling snow. My sister and I each had one brother glued to us sandwiched in the back seat with Danny, the youngest, in the middle. He was drinking a bottle and making noises to try to get back to sleep.

Michael and Raymond finally drifted off under the crock of a sister's arm. Bridie was making noises in the front seat. No one talked. The snow seemed to drive the car back. There were no other cars on the road. Mike drove on persistently. The chains clanked together. There was a bridge, a streetlight, some telephone poles and the constant wind and snow.

Bridie broke the silence with a louder noise. Then hardly breathing she said, "Mike, I don't know." We didn't know what she didn't know but we knew it was serious. The boys slept, Danny stirred and shifted in his seat. Everyone moved to fit him in.

Mike drove the car on through the snow until he saw the sign Wyman's. There was a steep unplowed hill up to Wyman's and he knew the car wouldn't go up that hill. He stopped at the bottom of the driveway and quickly went to Bridie in the front seat. She tried to struggle out of the door and couldn't move.

"I'll have to carry ye, Bridie, don't move. Ye'll hurt the baby. It's the only way. You can't walk."

Too weak to object Bridie leaned against him as he picked her heavy body up and carried her up the hill. Not a word was said to the children in the back seat. No words were needed. We cried quietly. No words just tears of relief. The darkness fell over us like a blanket, the snow gathered on the windshield, it began to get colder. But somehow, we were safe and warm, all huddled together.

Something happened that night. Some kind of awareness. Some understanding about birth, and about a woman and a man. It happened when Mike picked Bridie up to carry her up the hill. Somehow when she couldn't help herself, he'd found a way to help her.

That night, in the darkness, in the silent snow, it became very clear to me. You do need men and women to make babies, and to help each other when they can't help themselves. That night, my father's strength and love was the only thing to save her mother, and the new baby, and I knew it!

There is no choice--teaching happens!

On that snowy night, my mother and father had not thought of teaching me a lesson. They were simply involved in the constant process of teaching that belongs to being a parent. It's a process that goes on every day, every year, in times of peace, in times of war.

The curriculum that was set up that night was determined by what my mother and father thought they were--parents, husband, and wife. The lesson I learned was what I meant to them, how they loved their children and how they loved each other. The lesson was love! They had learned to love, and they taught love.

In spiritual teaching, we go to the very heart of the matter. Words are irrelevant. Words may coincide with the teaching but don't have to. What mattered on that snowy night in Maine is that my father picked my mother up and carried her the distance. In his mind it wasn't <u>too</u> far. She wasn't <u>too</u> heavy. He did it because he loved and believed in her, in the baby, in himself. Spiritual teaching reinforces what you believe about yourself. The self that you <u>believe</u> is real--that is the "self" you teach.

You teach what you think you are!

Just as I proved in my reversal of the "disruptive" Billy in the classroom, it's all about what I believe. If I go through life believing I am vulnerable, limited, and weak, I will teach vulnerability, limitedness, and weakness to everyone I meet. If I believe I am a powerful spiritual being, connected to God, A child of God. I will teach that truth.

Think of a time when you were not confident and tried to teach the world you were something you are not. Maybe you tried to show your friends you were something by wearing expensive clothes and driving an expensive car. Did you ever suspect you couldn't do a job but pretended you knew how?

When we don't have a secure spiritual identity, a deep sense of being loved by God, we might pretend we are of this world and teach what we are not. We might teach business executive, professional, lawyer, doctor, or Indian Chief. Whatever role we drown ourselves in, it's only a small part of our real identity-- our spiritual identity as a child loved by God.

Earlier in my life I became lost, forgetting the lessons of love taught to me by my parents and Mrs. Parson, sidetracked by material possessions and social status. For a few years, I saw myself only by the roles I played in the world.

My country club years

This was a time in my life when I didn't have a secure spiritual identity--a. time when I tried to present an image to the world, a time when I made decisions on appearances. In college, I met and married a man who had all the right credentials: right religion, social and financial status, family business, nationality, and education.

For the first few years we belonged to the "country club set" just as his mother and father had. It really was a phony world of self-aggrandizement, ego-building, and materialism. Both of us were led by our addictions and we drank too much, played too hard, and generally lived on the edge.

Now, when I think of those years, I remember how little I had on the inside. It was as if I was spiritually bankrupt. I attended church not to nurture me but to present an image of spirituality to the world. What was I teaching? Status and money! Consistent with my ego-based thinking, I gave back to the world a hollow empty shell of myself.

It was only when the family business failed, and we were financially bankrupt that the country club world came crashing down. Then, I began to grow spiritually. Our friends didn't invite us to their parties anymore--no status, no money. We dropped the country club membership after my husband's 32 years of consecutive "belonging". I went back to work teaching in a local high school. We didn't take our kids to the club pool in summer; we took them camping on an island in the Atlantic Ocean. We canoed the Allagash River instead of going on cruises and no longer felt controlled by the image of status and money. We had freedom to be something else. We didn't know what we would become yet, but the door was open to new opportunities.

Many times, people say they didn't know "who they were" until striped of all worldly possessions. Some spiritual teachers actually seek to be free of the hindrances of money and position. They seem to have learned that great understanding of self can come through what the materialistic world might consider adversity. I needed to ask myself the biblical question, "What profit is it to a man if he gains the whole world and loses his soul?" (Matthew 16:26 NKJV) When I heard those words spoken in church, I finally understood what they meant?

There are times today that I need to take an inventory and ask myself these questions: What motivates me? What takes up my time? How much of my world is tied to my successes? How much time do I spent promoting myself and worldly interests? What about spiritual interests? How much energy do I expend helping/loving others? Who am I? What do others mean to me? What do I teach?

What is the curriculum of the world?

Whenever anyone is so caught up in their job, earning money, their family traditions or even society itself, they tend to be following the curriculum of the world and tend to teach others what they are not. They are not only the job, the family, the society. These roles are only a small part of our real identity.

"Until you change your mind about who you are and understand your spiritual identity, you will find yourself teaching a curriculum of the material world which always leads to despair and death." (ACIM)

Working in a public school system for many years gave me the opportunity to get to know thousands of students. They became my teachers. Ironically, the ones with severe disabilities, with the most adversity in their lives, had the most profound lessons to teach. Two incredible examples were Sarah and Josh who had cerebral palsy from birth. I recount their stories here.

A Special Disability :"A CUP OF COFFEE"

The shocking news went through our school like a sudden tremor. It was Sarah, one of the East Conn Kids, the kids who have a special room upstairs. You know, the pretty one who couldn't talk--Sarah was in the cafeteria, with Chris, her aide, holding her hands, typing words on a talking computer. One of the kids asked her what she had always wanted to say, and she wrote "F------ you. I'm not stupid!" The kids loved it--poignantly, powerfully, she made her point with words you don't say in school.

When I heard the story, I cried. Remembering Sarah being led into the cafe, I thought of her bright colored lunch bag in one hand and the aide holding her firmly with the other. Once, she got away and came and hugged me. I never forgot that gesture. It was like she wanted to reach out of her body and touch someone in the world.

Sarah has Cerebral Palsy, and could not speak, write, communicate with facial expression, or body language, and had only peripheral vision. There didn't seem to be any way to test her cognitive skills, so it was assumed they were limited. Many tests had been tried over the years, but nothing worked. When they asked Sarah to point to a certain picture, she couldn't hold her hands steady enough to hit the picture.

Consequently, her early education was structured for a person of limited ability: no reading, no writing, spelling--nothing but Sesame Street and the flash cards her mother put up around the house. That's where Sarah was at 14 years of age--no formal education.

The breakthrough came in her freshman year when she began working with Chris, her facilitator, who directed her hands to the computer. She could think, and write thoughts. Then, Sarah was mainstreamed into regular classes with Chris at her side. I anticipated her senior year with eagerness and some trepidation--it would be my turn at having Sarah in my class. When her senior year came, it happened, I scheduled an interview with her and Chris, her aide, who held her hands as she typed. In one of our first sessions, I asked Sarah about what happened the very first time she typed out her first words.

"Who was there?" I asked.

"JOE, CHRIS, ME" The computer spelled out the BIG BLOCK LETTERS that I would come to know as Sarah's distinct voice.

"Why did you try? I questioned.

"I NOT KNOW. I JUST DID. I NOT SURE WHY I TOOK THE CHANCE. OR WHY PEOPLE TOOK THE CHANCE THEY DID BUT I'M GRATEFUL THEY DID."

The letters came out one by one and I felt giddy at being able to speak to the girl who was inside. She had a simple syntax without too much formal sentence structure, sometimes without punctuation, sometimes with misspellings. It was the voice of a child with the limited vocabulary, of one who had been denied direct inter-communication for fourteen years. It was the voice of someone who couldn't speak with her mouth, only her soul. She chooses her words carefully. She said only what she meant, and she was remarkably wise.

Also available

ABC's of Grief **by Christine A. Adams!**

    The **ABC's of Grief: A Handbook for Survivors** meets bereaved persons wherever they might be in the grieving process, providing snatches of meaning, hope, empathy, and understanding. This handbook is a product of the author's own grief experience. Confronting her loss, Christine Adams found that it was all right to grieve at her own pace: one day at a time, one thought, word, and letter at a time.

    The handbook's alphabetical format allows readers, or group leaders, to focus on any aspect of grief that suits them. If a reader becomes absorbed in "anger" or "anxiety," he or she can go back to reread those parts of the handbook and with each visit will find some new realization and meaning. Every section contains appropriate quotations, stories, and poems, written by survivors who found solace in writing. The information is useful at a time of grief, the encouragement by the author is soothing, and the poems and stories remind the reader that others have visited the same places in their grief process.

    Read more at Christine A. Adams's site.

    http://www.christineaadams.com/

About the Author,

Christine A. Adams, M.A., has been writing about issues of addiction, relationship, spirituality, and education for over 32 years. She has over 2,000,000 separate books and pamphlets in print with works published in 52 countries translated into 35 languages. Chris, an English teacher, was also formerly trained as an addiction counselor in 1986. However, most of her writing parallels her life experiences. Her early writings were about the alcoholic marriage, adult children of alcoholics, teen alcoholism, and sexual addiction. Then came books about spirituality, relationships, grief therapy and education.

In addition, she has produced 4 very popular Elf Help children's books: <u>Happy To Be Me</u>, <u>Learning To Be A Good</u>

Friend, Worry, Worry, Go Away, and God Made Us One By One. One of her best-known recovery books is the adult Elf Help gift book, One Day At A Time Therapy which is still selling in places like Taiwan, China, Portugal, the Netherlands, Austria, Sweden, Indonesia, and Brazil. Her other books include: Spirituality: A Life Force, Let Go, Let God, Teacher of God, Holy Relationships, and ABC's of Grief: A Handbook For Survivors. Other books include a fictional narrative, based on her years of teaching, called The School Factory, and romantic novel, September Love. Visit her at www.christineaadams.com

    Read more at http://www.christineaadams.com/.